God is My Friend

Learning to read · from the Bible ·

God is My Friend

By V. Gilbert Beers
Illustrated by Robert Boehmer

ZONDERVAN
PUBLISHING HOUSE
OF THE ZONDERVAN CORPORATION
GRAND RAPIDS, MICHIGAN 49506

Learning to Read from the Bible Series

GOD IS MY HELPER
GOD IS MY FRIEND
JESUS IS MY TEACHER
JESUS IS MY GUIDE

GOD IS MY FRIEND
©1973 By V. GILBERT BEERS
Second Printing—1974
Library of Congress Catalog Card Number 72-85562

Printed in the United States of America

What's in This Book

A Word to Parents and Teachers

Reading is basic. It may well be the most important skill your child will ever learn. Without reading, his life would be seriously limited.

For this reason, thousands of dollars are spent in your community to develop reading programs for your children and their friends. Thousands more are spent to provide quality reading materials so that each child can read at his proper reading level.

Those of us who are parents are grateful for this concern and for the wise investment of money in reading programs. We want the best for our children.

But some of us are disappointed. We are sorry to see so few basic reading materials which emphasize Bible and Christian truth. Of course, we cannot hope for the public school to provide such materials. These must be offered for the home, the church, the Sunday school, and the Christian day school.

These materials must help the beginning reader accomplish several important objectives. First, he should learn what the Bible says, within his own word and concept level. Then, he should understand how the Bible situation fits into God's plans and what important truths about God may be learned from that situation.

Third, he should learn what this means to him. How do God's plans for Abraham, or Moses, or Joshua, relate to God's plans for him? Fourth, he should understand what he should do about these truths which he learns.

This book seeks to meet all of these important objectives. Stories help the child understand what the Bible says. Following each story, there are questions which help the child relate the story he has read to God's plans for the Bible character and for him.

A section called "New Things for Me to Do" helps the child find simple ways to apply the truths he has learned. All of this application material is given in the child's own reading vocabulary.

This book may be used as a supplementary reading book in Sunday schools or Christian day schools. Many parents will find it helpful in family devotions, permitting the child to take an active part in reading devotional materials himself. Your child should also find time to read this book by himself in his own quiet reading time.

If this book will help your child learn more about God's Word, or help him develop good Bible-reading habits, then it will serve its purpose.

V. Gilbert Beers

Jesus
Gives Us
Something
New

Jesus Gives Fishermen Something New

"Put the nets into the water," Peter called.

"Pull," shouted John.

Two other men pulled on the nets. They pulled the nets to the boat. But there were no fish in them.

"I'm tired of fishing," said Peter. "We have worked all night. But we do not have one fish."

"I'm tired too," said John. "Let's stop."

The other men were glad to stop. They did not like to pull in the nets with no fish in them.

Peter and his friends were fishermen. They worked each day in their boats. They took some fish home to eat. They sold some fish to get money.

When fishermen did not catch fish, they had no fish to eat. They had no fish to sell. But they had to wash their nets even if they did not catch fish.

The men pulled the nets to the boat.
But there were no fish in them.

When Peter and his friends came back, they washed their nets by the sea.

"It's no fun to wash nets when we don't catch fish," said Peter.

But Peter and his friends did not stop working. Soon the nets were washed.

Peter looked up. "Here comes Jesus," he said.

"Look at all the people with Him," said John.

Jesus stopped near the water. He began to talk to the people. He told them many things about God.

The people came closer and closer. Soon there was no place for Jesus to stand.

"Let's go into your boat," Jesus said to Peter and his friends.

So Jesus went with Peter and his friends into the boat. Then Jesus talked with the people again.

"Now let's go fishing," Jesus said to Peter and his friends.

"We worked all night," said Peter. "We did not get one fish." But Peter and his friends always did what Jesus said.

Peter and his friends put the nets into their boat. They took the boat out on the water.

"Put the nets into the water," Peter called. "Pull," shouted John.

All the men pulled on the nets. This time the nets were full of fish.

"Let's go fishing," Jesus said.

This fish will help you think about God's work.

"Jesus made those fish come into the nets," said Peter. "Jesus can do anything. He is God's Son."

"I have some new work for you to do," Jesus said. "I want you to go with Me. I want you to help Me do God's work."

Peter and his friends were glad to do what Jesus said. They were glad to do God's work with Jesus.

New Words I Have Learned

anything   Jesus   Peter

something   God   John

                       fishermen

New Thoughts to Think About

1. What new work did Jesus give to His friends? Were they glad to do it?
2. What work can you do for God?

New Things for Me to Do

Cut out some paper fish. Write one of these on each fish. Ask Mother or Father to help you.

Tell others about Jesus.

Give money to God.

Help people who do God's work.

Take others to God's house.

Put the fish on your wall. They will help you think about your work for God.

Saul looked for people who followed Jesus. He wanted to hurt them.

Jesus Gives Saul Something New

"Let me go to the city," Saul said to some men. "Let me bring back the people who follow Jesus."

The men smiled. They wanted Saul to go to the city. They wanted him to bring back the people who followed Jesus.

The men did not like the people who followed Jesus. They wanted to hurt them. Saul wanted to hurt them, too.

"We will make those people stop following Jesus," Saul thought.

Saul wanted people to follow him and his friends. He did not want them to follow Jesus.

"Jesus died," Saul thought. "Why should people follow a man who died?"

Saul thought that Jesus was not God's Son. He thought that Jesus was only a man.

One day Saul came near the city. Soon he would find Jesus' followers. He would make them go back with him.

Suddenly the sky became very bright. It was brighter than the sun.

Saul fell down on the ground. He was afraid.
Someone called to Saul. Saul knew that this
Man was talking to him from Heaven.

"Why are you hurting Me?" the Man asked.

"Who are You?" Saul asked.

"I am Jesus," said the Man. "Stop hurting Me."

Saul was afraid. Jesus was living. He was talking
to Saul. Jesus must be God's Son if He was in
Heaven.

"What do You want me to do?" Saul asked.

"Get up," Jesus said. "Go into the city.
Someone will tell you what to do."

**Saul knew that Jesus
was talking to him.**

These letters will tell you about a new life.

Saul got up. He went into the city.

Now Saul did not want to hurt Jesus' followers. He knew that Jesus had made him a new person. Now Saul would live a new kind of life. Now he would do what Jesus wanted.

New Words I Have Learned

Saul   bright   die

Heaven   person   someone

                     sorry

New Thoughts to Think About

1. What did Saul do before he knew Jesus? Why? What did he do after he knew Jesus? Why?

2. Have you asked Jesus for a new life? Would you like to do that now?

New Things for Me to Do

Write the letters S A U L on some paper. They will tell you about the new life you may have.

S — Be **sorry** for bad things you do.

A — **Ask** Jesus to take them away.

U — **Use** your new life for God's work.

L — **Love** God and please Him.

Jesus Gives Lydia Something New

"Where can we find some people who love God?" Paul asked.

"Out by the river," a man said. "Some women are there. They talk with God."

**"Are you the women
who talk with God?" Paul asked.**

Paul and his friends walked out of the city.
They went to a place near the river.

"There are some women," one of Paul's friends
said.

Paul and his friends began to talk to the women.
"Are you the women who talk with God?" Paul
asked.

"Yes," said the women. "You may stay here if you wish."

Paul and his friends talked with the women. Paul told them about Jesus. The women had not heard about Jesus before. They were so glad that Paul had come.

One of the women was Lydia. She heard all that Paul said. She was glad that Paul told her about Jesus.

"Jesus will give you a new life," Paul told her. "He will make you a new person."

"I want Jesus to give me a new life," said Lydia. "I want Him to make me a new person."

So Lydia asked Jesus to give her a new life. She asked Him to make her a new person.

Lydia was so happy. She told all the people in her family about Jesus. They asked Jesus to give them a new life, too.

Now Lydia wanted to do something for Jesus. But what could she do?

"I have a big house," Lydia thought. "I will ask Paul and his friends to stay here. That will help them work for Jesus."

So Lydia asked Paul and his friends to stay at her house. They were very glad that they

**Lydia asked Jesus
to give her a new life.**

**When Jesus gives us a new life,
we like to go to God's house.**

could stay there. Now they would not have to look for a place to live. They could do more work for Jesus.

"Thank you," said Paul. "Thank you for sharing your beautiful house."

"Thank you," said Lydia. "Thank you for helping me to have a new life with Jesus."

New Words I Have Learned

family   women   Lydia
share   Bible   Paul

New Thoughts to Think About

1. How did Lydia get a new life? What did she do when she got it?
2. How can you get a new life from Jesus? What should you do then?

New Things for Me to Do

When Jesus gives us a new life, we should do new things. Which of these are new things?

Learn from the Bible.

Go to God's house.

Tell others about our new life.

Talk to God.

Good Friends
and
Helpers

David and Jonathan Are Good Friends

"Who are you?" King Saul asked.

The boy smiled at the king. He smiled at Prince Jonathan, too.

"My name is David," he said. "I take care of my father's sheep."

"My name is David," the boy said.

"You are a very brave boy," King Saul told David. "Not one of our soldiers would fight the giant. But you did. With God's help, you won."

"I want you to live with me and my son, Prince Jonathan," the king said.

David was very happy. He wanted to live with King Saul and Prince Jonathan.

"You will be my best friend," said Prince Jonathan. "I want to be your best friend, too."

Then Prince Jonathan gave David some of his best things.

"This will show others that you are my best friend," said Prince Jonathan.

David knew that people gave their best things to their best friends.

"I will be your best friend as long as I live," David said to Prince Jonathan. "Thank you for your best things."

Prince Jonathan gave David some of his best things.

That day David went to live with Prince Jonathan and King Saul.

David and Prince Jonathan never hurt each other. They always helped each other.

Everyone knew that they were best friends. David loved Jonathan. Jonathan loved David.

That is what God wants all His people to do. We should help and love each other.

Good friends help each other.

New Words I Have Learned

David   prince   fight
Jonathan   soldier·   everyone

New Thoughts to Think About

1. How did people know that David and Jonathan were friends? What should we do for our friends?
2. What do you do for your friends? What do your friends do for you? What does God want you to do?

New Things for Me to Do

Which of these should friends do for each other?
  Give each other something.
  Fight each other.
  Say something good.
  Help each other do something.

A True Friend for Jeremiah

"We do not like Jeremiah," some men told the king. "He says things that make our soldiers afraid. You must put him in jail."

The king did not like Jeremiah. He did not

like what Jeremiah said. But he knew that Jeremiah said what God told him.

The king wanted to put Jeremiah in jail. But he was afraid to do it. He was afraid of God. He was afraid his people would not like him.

**"You must put Jeremiah in jail,"
some men told the king.**

Then the king knew what he would do. He would let these men put Jeremiah in jail.

The men hurried away to find Jeremiah. Then they put him in jail.

The jail where they put Jeremiah was not like other jails. It was a big hole in the ground. The hole had mud in it. It was cold and dark.

Jeremiah was very sad in the dark hole. He began to talk to God.

"Please help me," Jeremiah said.

While Jeremiah talked to God, a man went to see the king. The man's name was Ebed-melech.

"You should not keep Jeremiah in that big hole," said Ebed-melech. "Jeremiah is God's helper. He has no food there. He will die."

"Take some men with you," the king told Ebed-melech. "You may pull Jeremiah out of the hole."

Ebed-melech took some men with him to the big hole. Then he called down to Jeremiah.

"Jeremiah!" Ebed-melech called. "We have come to take you out of here."

Ebed-melech helped to take Jeremiah from the hole.

Think of something you can do for a friend.

Ebed-melech and his helpers put some rope down into the hole. They gave Jeremiah some rags to put under his arms. The rags would keep the rope from hurting his arms. Then they pulled Jeremiah out.

"Thank you! Thank you!" Jeremiah said to Ebed-melech. "I have been asking God to send help. Now you have come. You are a true friend."

New Words I Have Learned

Jeremiah	mud	Ebed-melech
jail	dark	arm

New Thoughts to Think About

1. Why was Ebed-melech a true friend? What did he do to show it?
2. Are you a true friend to others? What do you do to show it?

New Things for Me to Do

What have you done for your friends this week? Think of one good thing you can do. Think of a time when you can do it. Then do it for someone. Be a true friend to a friend.

Now think of something you can do for God. Show Him you are His true friend.

Zacchaeus Finds a New Friend

Zacchaeus was very sad. He did not have many friends.

People did not like Zacchaeus. They did not want to be his friend.

"Zacchaeus cheats," some people said.

"Zacchaeus steals," said others. "We do not want a friend who cheats and steals."

One day Zacchaeus saw a kind Man. "Who is He?" Zacchaeus asked.

"He is Jesus," some people said.

"I want Jesus to be my friend," said Zacchaeus.

The people laughed. "Jesus will not be your friend," they said.

Many people had come to be with Jesus. Zacchaeus could not see Jesus now. He was too little. He could not see over the people.

"I want to see Jesus," Zacchaeus said. "I will

People did not like Zacchaeus.
They did not want to be his friend.

climb that big tree. Then I can see Him as He goes by."

Zacchaeus climbed a big tree. He watched Jesus come down the road with the people.

**"Come down from that tree,"
Jesus said to Zacchaeus.**

Then Jesus stopped under the big tree. He looked up. Jesus saw Zacchaeus in the tree.

"Come down from that tree," Jesus said to Zacchaeus. "I want to go to your house."

Zacchaeus was so happy. He smiled as Jesus walked to his house. He gave Jesus good things to eat.

"I'm sorry for the bad things I have done,"

Zacchaeus told Jesus. "I will not cheat or steal again. Please forgive me. I will do what You want now."

Jesus smiled at Zacchaeus. "I will forgive you," He said. "I will help you become a new person. I will be your friend. You will be My friend, too."

Zacchaeus was very happy. He had found the best Friend of all.

Why not ask Jesus to give you a new life?

New Words I Have Learned

Zacchaeus   steals   become

cheats   forgive

New Thoughts to Think About

1. What did Zacchaeus do to become Jesus' friend? What did Jesus do for Zacchaeus?
2. What should you do to become Jesus' friend? What will Jesus do for you?

New Things for Me to Do

Have you ever asked Jesus to be your Friend? Why not do that now? Tell Jesus you are sorry for the bad things you have done. Ask Him to forgive you. Ask Him to give you a new life.

God
Is
With
Me

Jacob sat by the fire
and ate some food.

God Is With Jacob

"Hurry," said Jacob's mother. "You must go away from home."

Jacob and his mother were very sad. Jacob could not live at home now. He had made his brother Esau very angry. Esau was so angry that he wanted to kill Jacob. So Jacob had to go away.

All day long Jacob went away from home.
He went until it was night.

When Jacob stopped, he made a fire. This
would keep animals away.

"Now it is time to eat," Jacob thought. So
Jacob sat by the fire and ate some food.

Then Jacob lay down to sleep. He thought of many things as he looked up at the stars.

"God is up there," Jacob thought. "He is looking at me now."

Jacob thought of his father and mother. He thought of his brother, Esau. He was sad that he had to go away from home.

"But God will help me," Jacob thought. "He will take care of me. But I wish He were near so He could talk to me."

Soon Jacob began to sleep. While he was sleeping, he had a dream.

A ladder went up from the ground. It went up and up, all the way to Heaven.

Then Jacob saw some angels on the ladder. They were going up and down on it.

God said something to Jacob while he dreamed.

"I am here with you," God said to Jacob. "I will be with you at all times."

Jacob saw angels going
up and down on the ladder.

Jacob sat up. He looked around. "God was here with me," he said. "He will go with me at all times."

Jacob thought of many things as he went on his way. But he thought most about the things God had said. He knew now that God was with him.

What does each thing on the ladder tell you about God?

New Words I Have Learned

Jacob   brother   church

Esau   ladder   dream

                angel

New Thoughts to Think About

1. How did Jacob know that God was with him? Whom did he see on the ladder? Whom did he hear?

2. How do you know that God is with you?

New Things for Me to Do

Make a ladder on some paper. On each step draw one of these: a Bible, a mother or father, a church, the world. Each of these helps you know that God is with you. Cut out the ladder and put it on your wall.

The people hurried away from Egypt.

God Is With His People

"Let's go," said the mothers and fathers.

"Where?" asked the children.

"We must hurry to get out of Egypt," the mothers and fathers said. "The king does not like us. He wants to hurt us."

So the children walked with their mothers and fathers. They hurried away from Egypt.

The mothers and fathers had lived in Egypt for many years. They had lived there with their children.

But now they had to go away. The king was very angry. He wanted to hurt them.

"Why does the king want to hurt us?" the children asked.

"The king made us work for him," said the mothers and fathers. "He made us do many things. But Moses talked to the king. He told the king that God wants us to stop working for him."

Some of the things Moses did hurt the king. Some of them hurt Egypt. This made the king very angry. He wanted to hurt Moses' people.

"Will God let the king hurt us?" the children asked.

"God will take care of us," said the mothers and fathers.

"But how do you know?" asked the children.

Suddenly some people began to shout. "Look! Look!" they said. "Look at that cloud!"

A big cloud came near the people. Then it began to move ahead of them.

"What is it?" the children asked.

"What is it?" the mothers and fathers asked, too.

Then Moses told them what it was.

"God is in that cloud," Moses said. "He wants

"What is it?" the children asked.

**Make a cloud that will
tell you something about God.**

you to watch the cloud. Then you will know that
He is here with us."

God's people were so glad that they could
follow the cloud. They did not know where they
were going. But God knew. And God would
show them where to go.

"Thank You, God," they said. "Thank You
for the cloud. We know now that You are with
us. You will show us where to go."

New Words I Have Learned

| Egypt | Moses | cloud |
| move | everywhere | ahead |

New Thoughts to Think About

1. How did God's people know that God was with them? How did they know where to go?
2. Would you like God to show you what to do? You should ask Him to each day.

New Things for Me to Do

Draw a cloud on some paper. Ask Mother or Father to help you. Write "God is with me everywhere" on the cloud. Cut out the cloud. Put it in your car when you go away. Each time you look at it, think about the words.

God Is With Joshua

"How can we fight that city?" Joshua's soldiers asked.

Joshua looked at the big walls. His soldiers could never climb over them.

"God will help us," said Joshua. "He will show us what to do."

God did show Joshua what to do. He told him how to fight the city.

"How can we fight that city?"
Joshua's soldiers asked.

One day Joshua walked near the city. His soldiers walked with him. They walked around the city. Then they went home.

The people in the city did not know why Joshua did this. They did not know that God had told him to do this.

The next day Joshua came back. His soldiers came with him. They walked around the city again. Then they went home.

The people of the city were afraid now. They thought Joshua was going to do something to hurt them.

Every day Joshua walked around the city. Every day his soldiers walked with him. Every day they went home. But they did not fight the city.

"What are they doing?" the people of the city asked. "Why do they walk around the city? Why do they go home? Why don't they fight us?"

One day Joshua walked around the city with his soldiers. But he did not go home.

Joshua and his soldiers walked around and around. They walked around the city seven times. Then they stopped.

The people of the city were so afraid. They knew that Joshua would do something now. But they did not know what.

Joshua began to shout. His soldiers began to shout, too.

Joshua and his men ran into the city.

The big walls began to shake. Then they fell down.

Joshua and his men ran into the city. The people of the city did not know what to do. They did not try to fight.

"God helped us take the city," said Joshua. "We could not do this without Him."

New Words I Have Learned

shake	seven	Joshua
try	pray	without

New Thoughts to Think About

1. Did Joshua need help to take the city? What help did he get?
2. When you need help, do you want God to help you? Do you ask?

New Things for Me to Do

Here is a new word to learn. When we talk to God, we **pray**. We should pray each day. We should pray when we need God's help. We should pray to thank God. We should pray when we are happy for the things God does. Write the word **pray** and put it on your wall. It will help you think to pray.

Showing
Kindness

David Is Kind to Mephibosheth

King David had everything he wanted. He lived in a beautiful house. He had many people to help him.

But King David was very sad. "I wish Jonathan was here," he said.

Jonathan had been David's best friend. But he had been killed by some men.

**King David was sad
when he thought about Jonathan.**

King David thought much about Jonathan. He thought about the good times he and Jonathan had together.

"I know what I will do," David said one day. "I will find someone in Jonathan's family. I will do something kind for him."

King David sent for a helper. "I want to find someone in Jonathan's family," he told the helper. "Can you do it?"

"I know a man who can do it," the helper said. "I will bring him to you."

The helper brought the man to King David. Then David told him what he wanted.

"I want to find someone in Jonathan's family," King David said. "I want to do something for him. Can you help me?"

"Yes," said the man. "I will help you find Mephibosheth. He is Jonathan's son."

Mephibosheth was afraid when he came to King David. He could not run very well. He could not even walk very well.

"Please don't hurt me," Mephibosheth said to King David. "I will do what you ask."

King David put his hand on Mephibosheth and smiled.

"I do not want to hurt you," he said. "Your father Jonathan was my best friend."

Mephibosheth was happy to hear what King David said. He was glad that King David was so kind.

He knew that King David loved his father Jonathan. He knew that King David loved God, too. That was why King David was so kind.

Mephibosheth was glad that King David was kind to him.

**How can you be kind
to someone in your family?**

"I will give you everything you need," King David said. "You may live with me in my house. You may eat with me every day."

Mephibosheth knew that he could never give much to King David. But King David was giving him many things anyway.

"Thank you! Thank you!" Mephibosheth said. "You are the kindest man I know."

New Words I Have Learned

everything   Mephibosheth   anyway

New Thoughts to Think About

1. Why was King David so kind to Mephibosheth?
2. If you know Jesus, should you be a kind person? Why?

New Things for Me to Do

Think about each of these people. Which of them should you be kind to?

    Father   Jesus

    Mother   A friend

    Someone who does not like you

    Others in your family

    Others in your church

The Bible tells us to be kind to all of these people.

Some Friends Are Kind to Saul

"We do not like what you say," some men told Saul. "We do not want to be your friends now."

Saul was sad when he heard the men say that. He had been their friend. Now he wanted to tell them about Jesus.

For a long time, Saul had hurt people who loved Jesus. He had even helped to kill some of them.

But Jesus talked to Saul one day. He called down to Saul from Heaven. He told Saul that He was God's Son.

Saul's old friends did not like him now. They wanted to kill him.

When Saul heard that, he stopped hurting Jesus' people. He began to work for Jesus.

Now Saul wanted his old friends to know about Jesus. He wanted them to know that Jesus was God's Son.

But Saul's old friends did not like what Saul told them. "If Saul is right, then we helped to kill God's Son," they said.

Saul's old friends had helped to kill Jesus. They did not want to think that they had killed God's Son. So they were angry because of the things Saul said.

"We must not let Saul say such things," the men said. "We must stop him."

Saul's old friends knew how they could stop him. They would kill him.

But Saul had some new friends now. These new friends wanted to help him.

"We heard some men talking," Saul's new friends said one day. "They want to kill you. They will try to kill you when you walk outside the city."

Saul's new friends helped him
go away to another city.

These friends knew that Saul must go away.
He must go to another city.

One night, Saul went with his new friends.
They went to the wall of the city. They climbed
to the top of the wall.

"Get into this big basket," Saul's new friends told him. "We will let it down to the ground. Then you can go away to another city."

Saul's new friends let the basket down. Then Saul got out of the basket.

"Good-bye," Saul called back. "Thank you for being so kind to me."

Then Saul hurried away to another city. He would not be hurt now. His new friends had helped him. They were glad to help a friend of Jesus who needed help.

**What do you do
to help your friends?**

New Words I Have Learned

old   outside   good-bye

New Thoughts to Think About

1. Why did Saul's new friends help him? Should Jesus' friends help each other? Why?
2. Should you help Jesus' other friends? Do you? What can you do?

New Things for Me to Do

Draw a basket on some paper. Ask Mother or Father to help you write these words on it.

Share with friends.

Pray for friends.

Give to friends.

Talk with friends.

Be with friends.

Work for friends.

We can do these things to help Jesus' other friends.

Dorcas, the Kind Woman

"Dorcas is such a kind woman," all the people said. "She helps so many of us."

Dorcas did many kind things for her friends. She made clothes for some. She gave food to others. She helped mothers when they did not feel well.

When Dorcas came,
she always made people happy.

When Dorcas came, she always made people happy. The boys and girls were glad to see her. So were the mothers and fathers.

"Dorcas is here! Dorcas is here!" the children would say. Then the children would watch Dorcas help the mothers and fathers.

One day Dorcas did not come to see the people.

"Where is Dorcas?" some of them asked.

"She is sick," said some others.

Dorcas' friends all went to help her. They wanted their kind friend to get well.

But Dorcas did not get well. Before long, Dorcas died.

How sad all her friends were! "What will we do?" they asked.

Then someone thought about Peter. "Peter can help us feel better," they said. "Let's find him."

Some of the people hurried away to get Peter. When he came to see Dorcas' friends, they were crying.

The people were so happy when Peter helped them.

"Our kind friend has died," they said. "Can you do something to make us feel better?"

Peter walked into the room where Dorcas lay.

"Let me be alone with her," said Peter. So all of Dorcas' friends left the room.

Peter looked at Dorcas. Then he talked to her.

"Dorcas, get up!" he said.

Dorcas began to move. She opened her eyes and looked around. Then she sat up.

Peter smiled as he took Dorcas to see her friends. How happy they were to see her.

"Thank you! Thank you!" they said. "Thank you for giving our kind Dorcas back to us."

All the people were happy. But Dorcas was the happiest of all. Now she could do kind things for her friends again.

New Words I Have Learned

feel   Dorcas   cry

sick   open

New Thoughts to Think About

1. What kind of a person was Dorcas? What kind of people did she help?
2. When people need help, what should we do? What do you do?

New Things for Me to Do

Think of someone who needs help. Who is it? What does he need? What can you do to help? What can your friends do? Do something to help that person soon. Ask your friends to help you, too. Pray for God to help you as you do this.

What These Stories Teach

Each story in this book teaches an important Bible truth, or doctrine. Each story also teaches an important truth about the child's daily living.

These two truths, or objectives, are often so closely related within a story that they may not be obvious to the parent or teacher. All objectives, doctrinal and present-day, are listed here so they may be clearly understood by the parent or teacher.

Story	Doctrinal objectives	Present-day objectives
Jesus Gives Fishermen Something New	Those who follow Jesus are to do God's work.	We should find several ways to work for God.
Jesus Gives Saul Something New	Jesus can give a new life to those who will accept it.	We should tell Jesus we are sorry for our sin and ask Him to give us a new life.
Jesus Gives Lydia Something New	When Jesus gives us a new life, our conduct should change.	We should look for new things to do for God when we become Christians.
David and Jonathan Are Good Friends	God wants His people to be good friends.	We should try to be friends with other Christians.
A True Friend	True friends sometimes help God answer prayers.	We should show that we are true friends by doing things for others.

Zacchaeus Finds A New Friend	Jesus wants to be our best Friend.	We should ask Jesus to forgive our sins and give us a new life. Then He can be our best Friend.
God Is With Jacob	God is with us everywhere.	We should recognize the presence of God with us.
God Is With His People	God goes before us in strange places.	We should be grateful that God is leading in unknown places.
God Is With Joshua	God helps us do things we could not do without Him.	We should pray for God's help when we need help.
David Is Kind to Mephibosheth	People who know God should be merciful, for God is merciful.	We should be kind to others who cannot repay us.
Some Friends Are Kind to Saul	Christians should be kind to other Christians who need them.	We should help other Christians who need it.
Dorcas, the Kind Woman	Christians should be kind to people in need.	We should help those who have special needs.

Basic Word List

Most of the two hundred and eighty-four words on this basic list will be familiar to your child. These words have come primarily from standard word lists used in public-school education and from some of the most frequently used words in basic reading textbooks.

With each Bible story, you will find a list of new words which are not found in this list. Later, a cumulative list of all new words is given.

Variants of a word are usually not considered new words in this book. These include words made by adding s, es, ies, ing, ed, er, est, iest, or ly. Thus, talks, talked, and talking are not considered new words since talk is on the basic word list.

a	because	cold
about	been	come
afraid	before	could
after	began	cut
again	best	day
all	better	did
alone	big	do
always	boat	does
am	boy	doing
and	brave	done
angry	bring	don't
animal	brought	down
another	but	each
are	by	eat
around	call	even
as	came	every
ask	can	father
at	car	fell
ate	care	find
away	catch	fire
back	children	fish
bad	city	follow
basket	climb	food
be	close	found
beautiful	clothes	for

friend
from
full
fun
gave
get
giant
girl
give
glad
go
goes
going
good
got
ground
had
hand
happy
have
he
hear
heard
help
helper
her
here
him
his
hole
home
house
how
hurry
hurt
I
if
I'll
I'm

in
into
is
it
it's
keep
kill
kind
king
knew
know
laugh
lay
learn
left
let
let's
letter
life
like
little
live
long
look
love
made
make
man
many
may
me
men
money
more
most
mother
much
must
my

name
near
need
net
never
new
next
night
no
not
now
of
on
one
only
other
our
out
over
paper
people
place
please
pull
put
rag
ran
right
river
road
rode
room
rope
run
sad
said
sat
saw
say

see	the	wall
seen	their	want
sell	then	was
send	them	wash
sent	these	watch
she	there	water
sheep	they	way
should	thing	we
shout	think	well
show	this	went
sky	thought	were
sleep	those	what
smile	time	when
so	tire	where
sold	to	while
some	together	who
son	told	why
soon	too	will
spell	took	wish
stand	top	with
star	tree	woman
stay	true	won
stop	two	word
such	under	work
sudden	until	world
sun	up	would
take	us	write
talk	use	year
tell	very	yes
thank	walk	you
that		your

New Word List

In each story throughout this volume, new words are shown in the section "New Words I Have Learned." New words are those included in that story, but not included in the basic word list.

The following is a cumulative list of those sixty-seven new words used in the child's reading material. Words used in the instructions to parents and teachers are not considered for either of these lists.

No more than seven new words are used with each Bible story. Sometimes a smaller number is used.

Because these are Bible stories, many of the words are "specialized vocabulary words" relating to the Bible. These specialized Bible words will help to acquaint your beginning reader with Bible names and terms which he should begin to know.

ahead	everything	mud
angel	everywhere	old
anything	family	open
anyway	feel	outside
arm	fight	Paul
become	fishermen	person
Bible	forgive	Peter
bright	God	pray
brother	good-bye	prince
cheats	Heaven	Saul
church	Jacob	seven
cloud	jail	shake
cry	Jeremiah	share
dark	Jesus	sick
David	John	soldier
die	Jonathan	someone
Dorcas	Joshua	something
dream	ladder	sorry
Ebed-melech	Lydia	steals
Egypt	Mephibosheth	try
Esau	Moses	without
everyone	move	women
		Zacchaeus